Alphabet Success
Keeping it Simple
My Secrets to Success

ALPHABET SUCCESS Copyright © 2014 by Tim Fargo.

DEDICATION

For Ed and Catherine:
You Just Kept Looking

TABLE OF CONTENTS

ST. PETERSBURG, FL, September 11, 2003 — First Advantage Corporation, a St. Petersburg, FL-based provider of enterprise and consumer screening solutions, announced its purchase of Omega Insurance Services, also headquartered in St. Petersburg. Omega conducts fraud investigations for insurers, third-party administrators and self-insured employers nationwide, and was ranked 92 on Inc. magazine's 2002 list of the 500 fastest growing private companies in the United States. Omega's investigative services, which will add a new business line to First Advantage's portfolio of services, are expected to generate in excess of $20 million in revenue in 2004.

Founded in 1996, Omega is a private investigation firm licensed across the United States that currently employs more than 200 full-time field investigators in addition to an in-house staff of more than 100 employees in St. Petersburg.

Omega serves its clients by detecting and exposing workers compensation, disability and liability insurance fraud through surveillance and other investigative activities.

"Omega's expertise in investigative intelligence is a perfect complement to First Advantage's success in using data sources and technology to mitigate risk," said Tim Fargo, president of Omega Insurance Services. "Our collective experience will bring added value to our clients and the industry. Omega is excited about the additional resources we will be able to offer to our clients as a First Advantage company while we continue to provide the same personal service and attention to detail that has made us successful."

I can remember a lot of things about the days following the selling of Omega Insurance Services – the company I had spent the better part of a decade building from the ground up – but the moment that stands out in my mind is when I went to withdraw some money from an ATM in downtown St. Petersburg. I took my card from the machine followed by the cash, and then patiently waited for the receipt to print. When the receipt slid out of the machine, I took a deep breath and looked at the balance.

It's not every day that your lifetime dream is confirmed on a scrap sheet of paper, but that's how it happened for me, standing there in the Florida heat, my eyes adjusting to the large sum written at the bottom of the receipt.

Selling Omega was a long and difficult process, at times agonizing and other times tremendously exciting. When I finally signed the dotted line to seal the deal, it was like finally reaching your destination after an extremely long journey. What people don't realize is that my journey didn't begin with Omega, it simply ended up being the last step towards achieving my goal.

Standing there at that ATM, I thought back to the times when it seemed like I'd never get to this moment.

I remembered the heaviness of failure and disappointment when I filed for bankruptcy in 1990. I remembered the Christmas party when my business partners filed a lawsuit against me for $10,000,000. I remembered all those huge moments of doubt and frustration where it felt like I'd never make it.

Now, seeing those numbers in my account, I knew I finally had what I always wanted. You see, I have honestly wanted to be rich for as long as I remember. Not because I wanted to lord it over anyone, not because life had been particularly hard for me, or I felt I had something to prove, but simply because I seriously admired the amount of freedom that the people I knew with money appeared to enjoy.

But it's easy to say I want to be rich, it's another thing to actually become rich. This can be said about pretty much anything you want in life. The thing is that people don't question what their life is about, what it is they truly want, and most importantly, how to realistically get there. The purpose of this book is to help you get to where you want to be. I'll never pretend to tell you that it'll be easy, nor will I pretend that you're guaranteed to get there, but I can say that by following the ABCs I've created, you'll be able to map out a concrete plan to move you towards your destination with confident steps.

Like I said, Omega was the final step on a long journey. I failed time and time again, but I kept moving forward until I got what I wanted. I remember back in 1992, when I was starting my PhD at the University of Arizona. After spending months doing research and studying, I came to a distinct realization. I immediately set up a meeting with my advisor. I sat across from her and I said, "If I work this hard in the private sector I'll be able to retire in ten years."

I was off by one year.

Damn it all.

I still have that ATM receipt to this day.

ABC
Always Be Committed

"An organization that is strong and stable and is ready to commit time, money, and patience will be more apt to reap rewards than the quick-hitting opportunist."

-   Richard Miller

*You know that view about optimists and pessimists based on how they look at a half-filled glass? To the optimist it's half full and to the pessimist it's half empty. Me, I say throw the glass out the window and start again with a drinking horn. This way you have no choice but to **Always Be Committed.***

At a Christmas function a couple of months after starting Omega in 1996, my partners gave me a surprise present – a notice of a lawsuit for $10,000,000. They were suing me, claiming compensation for a series of "wrongs", probably hoping the sum would be enough to scare me out of business. There was a lot going on psychologically I'm sure, as they served the notice to me personally, at this function – of all places – in front of my new clients. The act combined with the bill featuring that many zeroes was enough to make me furious. But if they

11

thought they were going to knock me out of the game, they were wrong.

I'll never forget walking over to them with fury and determination, shaking their hands, and saying, "You forgot to wrap it."

The drinking horn was lifted and it wouldn't go down again until the job was done.

What do I mean by the drinking horn? We tend to associate drinking horns with medieval banquets, or perhaps our friends the Vikings, but they go back to ancient Greece and beyond. They could be simple cow horns or long curled antelope horns decorated with silver work, but the key thing about a drinking horn is not its size or shape, it's the fact that you can't put it down.

This is something most people don't think about. Once you take the drinking horn, you're committed to it. It doesn't matter if you're an American enjoying its novelty, a civilised ancient Greek honouring a friend or a rampaging Norseman celebrating a victory, the idea of the drinking horn is that once it's filled you're going to drink the lot. You can't take a few sips and quietly put it back on the table because it will fall over. You're going to have to drink it all – preferably in one go – which is why drinking horns are often associated with toasting.

There are no half measures with drinking horns.

You know exactly where you are with a drinking horn; you're focused on downing that draught from the moment you wrap your hand about it. You might have some doubts about the wisdom of what you're about to do, you probably have some questions about where this is all going to lead but the fact you're using a drinking horn at all means you're going to put aside such thoughts and get on with the job in hand.

What that means is that the vessel itself becomes a statement of intent. Take your place at a banqueting table decked out with drinking horns and you know what you're in for before anyone so much as cracks a bottle or opens a flagon.

In the world of business, the winners aren't those deciding whether their glass is half full or half empty. Business winners reach for the drinking horn instead, and in many cases it's that commitment, right from the outset, that ensures their success.

In the days following when that drinking horn was lifted at the Christmas function, my brain was full of shock as thoughts and feelings stampeded through, ranging from the idea of abandoning it all to "How dare they?" But the action they had hoped would frighten me off turned out to be what it took to galvanize me.

I had precious little money to fight and I was going to need help. I asked all the local attorneys in Birmingham, Alabama who they reckoned was the smartest, meanest, best-connected litigator they knew, and when that one name kept coming up over and over, I knew who I was going to see next.

The lawyer's name was Will Hancock. He was everything they said he'd be and more. When I went to see him I told him exactly how little money my fledging company had. I also told him exactly what little chance there was of having any more money any time soon. However, what I did offer was that no matter what it took to find it, I would claw together the money it took to pay for his services. I was not going to walk away or risk losing my case for a question of fees.

Not that it mattered, as the U.S. Federal Court dismissed the case as being without merit. My former partners had failed to put me off my stride and if anything made me a harder, more committed player than ever before.

This experience taught me a couple of things. The first thing is that you should always come out with guns blazing when things get tough. Just as you lift the drinking horn to commit to your goals, you do the same to overcome adversity. The second thing is that if you are that kind of person who'll be raising the drinking horn, you're going to have to recruit some similarly committed friends and partners along the way.

Of course you don't have to be backed into a corner in order to show commitment. Without realising it, we are often put off our game and gently pushed into business practices we don't choose through peer pressure, or the difficulty of standing up and doing things differently to everyone else. It can be subtle or overt, but we are constantly surrounded by this sort of pressure, and it is often harder to deal with than the kind of head on challenge that fired me up in '96. So I like to take the example of the late Steve Jobs.

Jobs didn't just co-found Apple Computers, he

was a driving force behind the company. You can easily see how the company lost its way during the years when he left. With him back at the helm, Apple came up with such stunning products as the iPod and iPhone which totally rewrote the rules of the game for their markets. Now Jobs had an undoubted vision of what products should be like, but most importantly he didn't waver in his commitment to that vision.

Famously, Apple doesn't do consumer research. Traditional thinking says that a company making consumer products should consult users on their needs and then release updated products that answer them. This tends to result in a slow evolution of design.

Jobs didn't buy that. He once told Fortune magazine, "We do no market research. We don't hire consultants. The only consultants I've ever hired in my 10 years is one firm to analyse Gateway's retail strategy so I would not make some of the same mistakes they made."[1]

His approach was to skip that and stay true to a vision of design-led products: "It's not about pop

---

[1]

Morris, Betsy. "Steve Jobs Speaks Out." CNN Money . 7 March   2008. <http://money.cnn.com/galleries/2008/fortune/0803/gallery.jobs qna.fortune/3.html>

culture, and it's not about fooling people, and it's not about convincing people that they want something they don't. We figure out what we want. And I think we're pretty good at having the right discipline to think through whether a lot of other people are going to want it, too."

Jobs never faltered from that commitment to a personal vision and the results have been revolutionary not only in terms of the marketplace, but how we organize our lives. How many of you have a large music library sitting on your shelves at home? We are a material culture suddenly willing to invest in intangible products. Apple changed the way we consume and store music and they look to be doing the same with books.

This approach owes a lot more to the drinking horn than the half full glass.

So commitment is the conviction that it's right to fight for what you want – and the delivery that means you do that every day and every way that you find yourself being pushed in a different direction. If you have that strength then the question is not whether you will succeed, but when.

I remember one of my first job interviews. It was a good company and the job was perfect, but at $30,000, the pay didn't match up. During the interview, they asked me if I had any questions. I immediately said that the pay wasn't good enough. I'd only take the job for $40,000. Obviously they were taken aback by my request, but I countered with, "Look, if you're standing in a department store and there's a shirt that you really want for $40. You don't negotiate. You have only two choices: you either buy the shirt for $40 or you leave without it."

They offered me the job at $40,000.

So how committed are you?

And how can you make sure you get and stay committed?

Commitment is a process that you can't just jump into. To be truly successful, real commitment is actually a number of different commitments:

1.	Commitment to yourself.
2.	Commitment to your vision.
3.	Commitment to action.
4.	Commitment to others.

1. Commitment to Yourself

How often do you make promises to yourself and fail to keep them? Procrastinating less? Losing a bit of weight? Failing to lose that weight when you wanted doesn't necessarily mean you're a commitment failure, but it does suggest that either you didn't truly commit to the project, or else you're generally not really committed to yourself.

Giving up smoking? A pharmacist friend of mine would tell me that when someone came in asking about ways to quit smoking, he'd always ask, "Do you really want to quit smoking?" It's such a simple question, but what he'd find out is that most people didn't, but they had to for whatever reason. When they were done explaining their situation, he'd say, "I could recommend a dozen different products here for you, but none of them are going to do a thing unless you *really want* to quit. Until you're ready to make the promise to yourself, don't waste your money."

Really committed people follow through on even the little promises to themselves because they believe that if you don't commit then there's no point in making the promise.

2. Commitment to Your Vision.

What's your mission statement? No, not one of those mealy-mouthed boilerplate jobs that lazy corporations draw up to confuse the shareholders. I'm talking about clear, real world terms that define what it is you're all about and what you want from life. Steve Jobs' personal mission statement would probably revolve around pursuing design-led innovation.

What's yours?

Because if you don't have one, and I mean one you really believe in, then you're not going to be able to commit to it and that means you're not going to get it. Simple as that.

3. Commitment to Action.

There's no point in being committed to a vision if you're not equally committed to making it a reality.

Big dreams are always daunting so break it down – identify each step on the way to the big idea and draw up a schedule of exactly where you're going to start and when. The world has plenty of dreamers but it's the doers that shape the planet. We'll be looking at the difference when we get to **PQR**.

4. Commitment to Others.

Did you notice the 'we' in that Steve Jobs quote from before? As in "We figure out what we want. And I think we're pretty good at having the right discipline to think through whether a lot of other people are going to want it, too." Jobs recognized that success comes from getting other people to fall in behind your dream and help make it happen. Real commitment must also mean commitment to the people who are part of your process. Jobs recognizes his staff's ability and encourages them, which in term means they commit to the dream. I'll be talking more about this later at **GHI**.

Do Try This At Home

If you've ever failed to deliver on a promise to yourself on the first attempt, but later succeeded, the chances are that you didn't really commit to the project first time around. Maybe you liked the idea of losing a bit of weight, but it needed that wedding/reunion/forthcoming film role to make you realize that now is the time. So go back to your list of goals (you do have one, right?) and go through them working out whether you are really committed enough to see them through. If you're in doubt then think what it would take to raise your level of commitment. If the answer is that there is no answer, then take that item off your list because you're just kidding yourself. Of course, if it really hurts to accept that and drop this project, you might want to start at step one again and consider how much you're prepared to commit after all.

DEF
Don't Ever Forget
(to say thank you)

"Feeling gratitude and not expressing it is like wrapping a present and not giving it."

- William Arthur Ward

There's an old saying that it's the squeaky wheel that gets the oil, and in business that means that most of our attention and effort goes to the more vocal and demanding clients or staff. That said, however important it may be to keep those squeaky wheels turning smoothly, don't ever take the quiet ones for granted. Take a moment to think of all the clients, employees, and suppliers who have helped your business succeed without feeling the need for hissy fits, histrionics, or hamming it up. Now think about how you're going to go about thanking each and every one of them. **Don't Ever Forget***, because your success counts on it.*

21

There is no end of studies that compare the cost of client acquisition with that of client retention. Or the cost of finding new staff after old ones leave, but while many of us pay lip-service to the idea of keeping people content, most of us completely miss out on the basics needed to do so. Management consultants will tell you that 'customer-focused strategies and operating models' are the answer to keeping companies profitable. They'll talk about understanding changing customer behaviours, about becoming 'customer-centric', about predicting future needs, and fine-tuning channel strategies and innovative marketing campaigns.

And they'd be right – these are all fine and intelligent responses to a volatile economy and butterfly consumer behaviour. Look at all of these things, by all means (far be it from me to take the bread out of consultants' mouths), but before you do anything else, take a look at the cost benefits of simply saying 'thank you'.

There's nothing quite so customer-centric as a personal acknowledgement of their importance, and in an age where Customer Relationship Management is largely regarded as something to be handled by the technical department, there has never been a better time to bring the personal touch into play.

When it comes to showing your thanks, you need to focus on these four groups:

1. The Customers.
2. The Complainers.
3. The Staff.
4. The Waterworks (probably not what you think).

1.   The Customers

Technology has given us a whole new weight to the art of saying thank you – but probably not in the way you think I'm about to say. Yes, I know that email/Instant Messaging/Twitter all mean that I can now blurt out my gratitude to hundreds of customers with little more than the touch of a button, but it's precisely because electronic expressions are so quick and easy that the handwritten note has developed another dimension. It's nice to get a dashed off email saying 'thank you', or at least it's nicer than getting nothing at all, but as online communications become the norm, the old fashioned ways stand out all the more for their simple strength.

When was the last time you got a handwritten note in a hand-addressed envelope? Probably back in the days when your first love sent you miss-spelt missives with SWALK scrawled across the back (you lucky thing, you).

With Omega, we always sent handwritten, hand addressed with normal (non corporate) thank you cards for every stick of business we got. GK Chesterton once said that "thanks are the highest form of thought, and that gratitude is happiness doubled by wonder." Spot on. We so rarely give or receive thanks properly that getting them is a wonder in itself. Realising that someone has gone out of their way to do it personally, not just by dashing something off on a keyboard most certainly doubles that happiness.

Don't take my word for it – just think about how you feel as a customer yourself. When was the last time you bought products or services and a few days later got a follow up note thanking you for your purchase? A real one? Wouldn't it make you feel just a little warm inside? Wouldn't it be the kind of little thing you mentioned to others when talking about the business?

Now I've seen the statistics same as you have and we all know that the amount of consumer choice has never been greater and your next competitor is only a mouse click away. But the majority of customers who leave a company don't do so just because the rival has a better special offer this week, they do so because they think that the company doesn't care about them so why would they care about the company?

In a 2010 article at *Aardvark Media*[2], there was a piece entitled "The next big thing - Thank you notes from CEO's" in which the writer was marvelling at the fact that a software company's CEO had sent a hand written letter to thank them for ten years as loyal customers. The piece went on to ponder whether this was the "emergence of a new trend of personal notes thanking customers personally for their business; the power of the handwritten note trumping the less-than-personal, manufactured emails that are automatically churned out by eCRM systems the world over."

I couldn't agree more, it's just that Omega had been doing that since 1997.

With Omega, another highly effective time-worn technique for thanks proved to be taking a client out to dinner (in itself a rarely refused gesture) and at an opportune moment saying in a serious tone, "I need to tell you something." Allow for a sufficiently dramatic pause and then say, "I really need to thank you for your business. It means a great deal to me and everyone at Omega

---

[2]   Jones, Christopher. "The next big thing - Thank you notes from CEO's." *Aardvark Media Blogs*. 6 January 2010. <http://blog.aardvarkmedia.co.uk/2010/01/06/the-next-big-thing-thank-you-notes-from-ceos/>

that we have earned your trust."

The result was incredible both in emotion and business. You'd be surprised how even hard-boiled customers will suddenly open up when they are simply thanked face to face. Sure some will just say 'you're welcome' and get back to the soup but most will become ecstatic that you bothered to say thank you in person and to make a big deal of it. I don't know how many such conversations have immediately turned into planning for future business, but there's no doubt in my mind that this simple step has been a huge factor in retaining clients and transforming customers into partners for the future.

The trick is just to say it. This isn't meant to suggest throwing out thank-yous insincerely at the drop of the hat, but rather to take the opportunity to show your appreciation for the people who are integral to your success. If the person across from you has helped you to get you where you are right now – no matter how small the contribution – then tell them how grateful you are.

2.   **The Complainers**

No, I'm not mad.

It's natural to try to avoid customers who complain but it's not the way forward if you want your business to succeed. Here's the thing; most customers don't complain – they just walk. The ones who complain might just be bellyachers but they still care enough about the relationship with your company that they come to you when they have a grievance. These are exactly the people you should be thanking. Not because they bent your ear, but because they came to you. So write them a thank you for bringing problems to your attention, and for expressing their frustration. Point out that you do care (the letter itself goes a long way towards this) and say what you are doing to put things right and to ensure their patronage continues into the future.

You know it makes sense – but do you really do it?

3.   **The Staff**

I can hear you thinking, okay, thank the customers. Got it. So far so good. But real gratitude and its expression is not something to hoard just for the people who sign the cheques. Take a long hard look around you and think how many peoples' efforts go into making your life a success.

No, I'm not talking about an Oscar acceptance speech. If you're tempted to burst into tears and thank your parents, your god, your scriptwriter and the key grip, then put the book down, get a grip of yourself and try again. Try – just as an idea – starting with your staff.

Staff loyalty is absolutely vital to business success, but very few staff get thanked for their input – even when it has been noted by their managers. There are lots of reasons why people don't thank their staff, ranging from not really noticing/appreciating their input, to feeling embarrassed about thanking them, or even afraid that thanking them will lead to them asking for pay raises.

Well, put all of those reservations to one side.

If you don't really think you have anything to thank your staff for, then ask if your business would still be running if they all walked out tomorrow. If you really feel you can do without them, either you're in a unique line of business or you're not really appreciating what they do. If you're embarrassed about thanking, then do it by letter (handwritten, naturally), and if you think they will ask for more money, well, that's a whole other issue and one to take on its own merits – but it certainly shouldn't stop you from saying 'thank you'.

At Omega, we always had frequent contests for sales with prizes like trips, days off, or experiences of some kind (try tank driving or paragliding). It worked so much better than just handing out cash bonuses and if you want to know why, try reading *Predictably Irrational* by Dan Ariely. By making the prize an experience rather than a figure in a bank balance, you generate a personal response in people which leaves them feeling more inclined to be loyal to the company and more loyal to you. Just give them cash and they will end up simply comparing figures with rival companies – just ask the banking companies how that works.

But sometimes there are situations where a contest won't cut it. I got this note from an ex-employee that I savour:

> "One memory I treasure, Tim, is one you probably don't remember. We were working late and I found out another report had to be edited before I could leave for the day. We sent out for a six pack, then while we're drinking our beers at work, you came by and opened your wallet and gave us each a $50 bill. You knew we were tired and frustrated and that was a great way to say thanks. No hollow praise. No plaque with a trite phrase engraved on it. You opened your wallet and thanked us. I still remember that day."

Of course, if you hand out money all the time then not only do you go broke but you get taken for granted. The reason why that employee remembers that day is not so much that it was rare (I'm not that mean), but because it was spontaneous and heartfelt.

The point here is sometimes just saying thank you isn't enough. Sometimes you have to show them by using more than words. Either way, it's all about **DEF**.

4.   **The Waterworks.**

Most companies organise bonuses of some kind for their sales staff, but most of them don't bother for the lower profile (sometimes nearly invisible) staff from admin, accounting, HR, and IT – the people whom I lovingly referred to as the waterworks as no one ever calls them unless there's a problem. If you only thank sales staff, you not only don't understand how companies run but you are also risking creating envy and divisions within your own. What we've done is set up functions as a thank you to the valiant invisibles at which I make a point of personally thanking them for making the whole thing work so seamlessly. It all boils down to 'Live with an attitude of gratitude.'

Think you're too important for that?

There's a tale of a certain US presidential candidate who took a box of thank you cards with him for the entire campaign trail. He would make a point of immediately penning notes to the workers as he went along day by day and many of them reported that they believed it made the difference in morale that won him the presidency.

Which one was it?

George H. Bush (no, definitely not W).

If it worked for him...

Do Try This At Home

Put the book down now and draw up a list of a minimum of five people who have made a difference to your business this week. Before you rush to gush to them, think carefully about whether they were part of a team effort and who else may be behind their success. Now write to each of them and thank them for that effort being precise about what strengths and results you are so appreciative of. Then send out the notes. Let them take a little time to settle in and then once those staff are secure in their value, find out who they have appreciated (thank them first – don't let them think you're digging to see if they're taking credit for others) and suggest that they pass your thanks on to those individuals. With a bit of luck your own gesture will turn into a snowball of gratitude – and eventually a virtuous circle.

GHI
Getting Highly Inspired

"The greatest danger for most of us is not that our aim is too high and we miss it, but that it is too low and we reach it."

- Michelangelo

If you can't get excited about your business, then how on earth can you expect anyone else to be? If you're not excited by what you're doing, then you won't be motivated and if you're not motivated, you're never going to be able to power up the people around you. In order for this to work, it's going to involve you **Getting Highly Inspired**.

Theodore Roosevelt used to say "People ask the difference between a leader and a boss. The leader leads, and the boss drives." Don't fall into the trap of becoming a donkey driver, plodding towards your goal at the same speed as the long-suffering beasts of burden you drive along with you. All too many people fall into the trap of doing a job because they allow the daily

33

drudge to block out their dreams.

Never let that happen to you.

Make sure you know what fires you up because you want to be racing ahead of the front of the pack, not rounding up the rear grumbling and waving the whip. Now this is going to sound a little strange, but hear me out before you judge me. Once upon a time, I used to occasionally drive to a Ferrari dealer just to sit in the black leather bucket seats and look out over a curving fire-engine red bonnet. It made me more excited about the possibilities of Omega.

You're probably thinking that makes me a little sad or at least an overgrown schoolboy.

Well, let me tell you a little more.

We are all motivated by different hopes and dreams, but a lot of us make it through life without real clarity about what we want. Oh sure, if we're pressed we say a little more money might be nice but it's all a bit vague.

Listen to a few of those interviews with lottery winners – when they're asked what they intend to do with the money, 90% of them reply that they're going to pay off the mortgage, settle the credit cards, go on a holiday and, erm, well it runs out there because that's as far as they've thought about the subject. And these are the ones who now have all that money in their hands.

For **Getting** **Highly** **Inspired**, I recommend:

1. Using symbols to inspire you,
2. But never confusing the symbol for what it stands for.

In order to better understand what I mean, consider the following two stories.

The Ferrari

Like I said at the beginning, I have honestly wanted to be rich since I was a boy. I seriously admired the amount of freedom that the people I knew with money seemed to enjoy. In order to help motivate me to reach that freedom, I used to pay a monthly visit to a Ferrari dealership in Saint Petersburg and sit behind the wheel of a 348. I would imagine myself cruising through town in it with my wife by my side and the wind in our hair. Then, with that motivation in mind, I sat down with an Excel spreadsheet to work out exactly how much money I would need to be able to afford that set of wheels.

If you think you've guessed the end of that story you're probably wrong. I never did buy the Ferrari because when I had made the money I enjoyed the freedom not to go for a symbol that costs more than most homes. The point was never that car – it was the motivation it represented. It was a symbol, and it's important not to confuse the symbol with what it stands for.

Mexico

Another story of what makes me tick dates back to a six month trip I took to Mexico. I found myself in Oaxaca at Monte Alban - the site of a great ceremonial centre built on a flattened mountain top by the Zapotec people. I'd had the time to scuttle around all day exploring the place and was now resting in the shade, exhausted but happy. At which point the tour buses turned up and from them poured throngs of pensioners. Don't get me wrong, I have nothing against the pensioners and am deeply impressed that they spent their time visiting such sites at all but there was no way, given their fitness level or their time schedule that they could see the site. Instead they essentially disembarked, trudged to the centre of the site, and were packed back onto the bus.

Now there's nothing uncommon in that scene, but it provided me with an epiphany. No way was I going to wait for my golden years to see the world. No way was I going to toil my whole life and count on packing in what makes life worthwhile into the years left to me when I had finished serving a career, a boss, or some other company.

So there you have it – a combined motivation to get the good things in life (and an awareness of the math behind getting there), plus an absolute determination to get what I wanted in time to enjoy it while the enjoying was good.

Which is why when I started Omega, the goal was always to grow it as fast as humanly possible (or inhumanly, I wasn't bothered) – and then sell it. It sounds simple, but most people starting a company do so for a whole heady cocktail of reasons including interest in that line of work, pride, self-fulfillment, lack of other choices, you name it. Even the ones that think they want to sell out fast have rarely put together the exact goal (How fast? How much?) or the spreadsheet that shows them how to get there. That was what a Florida Ferrari dealership and a Mexican trip did for me, and for a long time, I kept a picture of the 348 in the top drawer of my desk just to remind me.

And just to make life interesting, I had a terrible credit rating (that filing for bankruptcy in 1990 sure didn't help) and was going to have to beg and borrow my business off the ground. But if you have the commitment you will keep going forward and the curious thing is that if other people sense that you are that clear about your motivation, they start lining up to come with you for the ride – partners, staff, and yes, even bank managers all actually want to run with leaders, not trudge with the donkey drivers.

If you have the drive, you apply a little creativity, and you have nothing to lose, the most amazing things can happen. In some cases I found the best thing to do was simply to look people in the eye and tell them straight, "I may not be the quickest to pay you, but you will be paid."

And without fail, they were.

So the first stage is definitely to fix on what it is that makes you tick and then use that to fire yourself up. That then gets you to the second stage which is to get others to believe in you and want to run the race with you. Which might even be all you need. But just to be sure of success, there's another stage – helping your people find what fires them up because once you're all shooting for the stars that's when the fireworks really begin.

Pretty much everybody wants to make their lives better. It's just that like those lottery winners, a lot of people get stuck into thinking that doing better means reaching for the next rung up the company ladder instead of thinking about which direction they want to climb. So make it part of your role to mentor people, which means going beyond showing them how better to do the job you gave them and thinking more keenly about how their own self-development is going to get them where they'd like to go.

That's the key to inspirational leadership.

If you treat people like work machines, you get a workplace full of tools. If you treat them to think and grow, you will get a workplace full of fired up staff who can take your company to places maybe you hadn't even thought of yourself yet. It all starts with asking a simple question – ask people what makes them tick; what their goals are. Listen carefully to the answers because if everyone just says what they think you want to hear then it doesn't mean you've chosen them well, it might mean they're not thinking for themselves. If they aren't running with you because that's where they want to go, then no matter what they say, they won't be truly on board with your projects.

Does that sound like risky advice? Encouraging your staff to think about what they want to get out of this (ad)venture for themselves?

Well, it shouldn't be. Not if you know exactly what it is you are after yourself. People respond well to managers who stop being bosses and start being leaders. They go the extra mile if they genuinely believe that your success is their success and vice versa. It's a classic hallmark of the insecure boss to be afraid of encouraging staff to think and dream for themselves. It might have worked for nineteenth century mill owners, but these days if you are dedicated to following your dream you will almost certainly need other inspired people around you to help fuel and fulfil that vision. Of course, it could just turn out that as you start to ask the question you find that you don't have the sort of people you want to have working for you. The simple truth is that it's better to find out now, and know what has to be done about it than to carry on driving donkeys. Don't settle for second best, don't let anyone else think that's what you're doing, and don't let them settle for anything but their dreams either.

Do Try This At Home

Pencil in daily time for each person who reports to you directly.

If you've got your motivation sorted, you should be an inspiration in any case so why not expose others to it. Give staff real time to talk about what they want to do instead of just calling them in when things go wrong or you're about to drop something new into their workload. For those that you can't meet one on one with every day, think about weekly, or at a pinch, even quarterly meetings dedicated to performance development and make it clear that these are not blame sessions but a chance to discuss how things can be better.

TIM FARGO

JKL
Just Keep Looking

"Vision is the art of seeing what is invisible to others."

- Jonathan Swift

*Remember what I said about absolute commitment. **Always Being Committed** means never taking no for an answer, never backing down from a challenge and always insisting on giving it your best shot. But be careful. A lot of people confuse the **Alphabet Success** with just putting their head down and charging blindly.*

Don't.

*Instead **Just Keep Looking** around you to see if there isn't a better way in.*

The idea of **Just Keep Looking** is a combination of iron tenacity and a healthy dose of creativity. Ever seen a fly repeatedly trying to get out through a screened window, when two feet away there is an unscreened window they could

43

buzz through effortlessly? Don't be the fly. Look around, think about different ways of approaching and see if you can't find a new door. That door could be a person, a technique, a qualification, or simply some way of sticking out enough that you get noticed. Tenaciousness is an admirable quality, but if it isn't teamed up with intelligence and imagination it's likely to lead to spending serious energy for no tangible result. Spice up your commitment with imagination and a little lateral thinking and what you have is a killer cocktail.

I once had a client whose favourite trick was to agree to an appointment only to refuse to see me after making me wait at her office. At first I found it annoying, and when it happened again I felt it was downright rude, but by about the fifth time I was determined to get through that door.

So the next time I was scheduled to spend an afternoon polishing her waiting room furniture with my hindquarters, I tried a different tack. It's standard practice to take a trinket or small gift as a form of introduction but I wanted something that was genuinely impossible to ignore. So I stopped by a local garden centre and bought a nine foot (3 metre) palm tree which proceeded to wave softly in the breeze as it hung out the back window of the car on the drive to her office.

Obviously the tree was bigger than me, and

better yet, it was sufficiently big that once installed in the waiting room it was not going to be an easy matter to get it out again. I like to think I was sending the same message about myself.

Certainly the receptionist was dumbstruck as I arrived with my one-man rainforest. Without taking her eyes off me (us?) she picked up the phone, announced my (our) arrival, and added that my potential contact really needed to come out to see what it was I had with me. Little Miss Wait-And-See was sufficiently intrigued by that to leave her office and from the moment she turned the corner and found herself greeted principally by a plant (with me tucked away in the foliage) she burst out laughing.

I had found a different door and we began to do business together.

I'm a great believer in presents, just as I am in saying 'thank you'. In fact, **DEF** could easily be applied to presents, as they come in many shapes and their value is often in how you choose to use or offer them.

For example, one day we found ourselves carrying out a routing check on a lady who was claiming disability allowances for a back injury. Claims companies don't like paying out for spurious claims so it was part of the job to drive by to see if she was indeed at home rather than, say, break-dancing at the local mall or turning up as quarterback for the local college team.

When our investigator pulled up the first thing that caught his eye was not the lady we were asking after but rather her husband. Preliminary checking had shown that her husband was also on disability benefits for bilateral carpel tunnel syndrome. Bilateral carpel tunnel syndrome is a particularly nasty affliction that stops you using your wrists and I wouldn't wish it on anyone, which is what made it all the more striking that the lady's husband was sweeping the patio with a vigour not normally seen from able-bodied men doing household chores. Now the husband wasn't our concern since the company he was claiming from was not one of our clients, so the investigator called me for instructions. I didn't have to think too long. The other company might not have been a client but I wasn't going to pass up a chance to open a new door so I told our guy to film this near-miraculous feat of spring cleaning.

With the tape safely on my desk, I called the secretary of the claims manager in the other company. I explained to the secretary that I had something I was 100% sure he would like to see and, predictably intrigued, he picked up the phone. When he learnt what it was he offered to pay us handsomely for our time but declined and said I'd send him the tape for free if he'd just give us a six month trial period on their vendor rotation. He got his tape, we got our chance, and they remained a client of ours to the day we sold the business.

The key point here is that at one point in the deal we were being offered some serious money for work we'd already done and the temptation would have been to take that and pat ourselves on the back for being so smart. That, however, would have meant missing the opportunity that was there to go for the bigger prize and gain a new client. Money, or short-term results often blind people to the fact that there is another way in to be had if that short-term gain is parleyed into a longer-term advantage. It's all about whether you're looking for a quick buck or a way into a new market.

One of my favourite approaches has always been to try and open a door by making it a no-brainer for the doorkeeper. For example, I was forever approaching potential clients with the offer that if we failed to deliver on the promised level of performance then not only would they not have to pay a penny but I would leave them alone and never again darken their door.

It's hard to say which part of the deal was the more attractive; guaranteed delivery, a free ride, or just getting to see the back of me but whatever the aspect that appealed most the overall package of the promise worked like a treat. The flip side of the deal was that if we delivered as promised we went onto their list of approved vendors. What's not to like about a deal like that? I knew we could deliver, but again, there are lots of businesspeople out there know that their companies can do what they offer. The difference was that I made the experiment as painless as possible for the potential client and put myself on the line in the process. The offer, and the passion with which it was delivered, spoke volumes about my belief in what we could do. It did so in a way that not only convinced the person across the desk from me, but just as importantly also gave them a strong logical argument to use with the people they reported to.

Never forget that business is competitive. One way or another you're always up against the other guy, even if you don't happen to have the slightest idea who the other guy is or even what business he's in.

That doesn't mean you have to get all paranoid and wander around looking over your shoulder for the competition, but it doesn't mean you should make it easy for them either. The simplest way of making yourself an easy target is to stand still and do the same thing. Markets change, clients move to other locations, new business models come into play. A successful business is always looking for what comes next, always embracing growth, and always absolutely sure there is another door coming up if you just know how to recognise it.

Do Try This At Home

The first step in finding a way through a wall is accepting that there is a wall there in the first place. So take a long hard look at where you and your business find yourselves right now. Could things be better? More successful? Could you be a step closer to your dreams? OK, so what's standing in the way? Do you need more investment? Better clients? Some fresh blood? Partners? Whatever it is, be absolutely honest and think about those things that you know in your heart of hearts aren't where they should be, but don't look likely to change any time soon. Now think carefully about where a doorway could be made in that wall and what shape that door might take. Is it a change in attitude? A person? A shift in strategy? Or is it simply coming at the same old problem from a different angle? If you're still stuck then ask yourself if pride/shyness/fatigue is stopping you from asking for a third party point of view. Sometimes a fresh pair of eyes is just what you need to sharpen up your own ability to see.

MNO
Make Notes and Observations

"You see, but you do not observe. The distinction is clear."

- Sherlock Holmes

*You don't have to be Sherlock Holmes to find huge value in little details, you just have to remember to write it down. Sweating the small stuff may be out of fashion but noticing it, allowing you to **Make Notes and Observations**, is often the secret to success when it comes to how you get on with clients and colleagues.*

Way too often we learn something about people around and us and think to ourselves 'that's interesting' then promptly forget all about it. It's like someone rootling through an attic, chancing on something eye-catching then putting it back in the pile and moving on. Ask any good writer about their craft, and they'll mention having a notebook to write down their ideas. Some of them even have one sitting next to their bed in the event they wake

51

up in the middle of the night with an idea. No matter how inspirational a thought is, no matter how amazing the idea is, life is full of distractions, and chances are you're not going to find it again back in that pile of other things.

The problem is that we both overestimate our memories and underestimate the importance of the details. Writing things down seems such a petty habit and most of us stopped keeping diaries when we were kids. Yet while we'd all agree on the importance of keeping in touch with clients, partners, and colleagues we are all happy to rely on the vagueness of memory to do the job. Oh ok, perhaps you might note down a birthday or two, but what about their kids'/grandkids'/dog's names? It's a funny thing that CRM (Customer Relationship Management) is all the rage when it comes to companies keen to record every touch point with a client, but we don't apply the same logic to our own personal transactions.

Time to start.

Given how easy it is now to note, store, index, and access information it's a bit primitive to just to leave it to luck and memory when it comes to the details of the individuals who make up your working day. We know how embarrassing it is to forget the name of someone's partner, and we know how easy it is to use a computer/PDA/smartphone to keep a record of it so there isn't really much excuse. Being the person who remembers the details isn't just about winning brownie points (though they never hurt) – it's also the concrete proof that you notice, that you care, and that other people matter to you. If you have that attitude to others you'll find that it comes back to you.

Many companies mumble the CRM manta but typically it means that they are trying to keep track of the touchpoints when a customer contacts a company. That's certainly better than all those companies that don't know that the person their sales staff is talking to is also the same person who has spent an hour this morning wailing at customer services. It's not enough though because it reduces people purely to the mechanics of their contact with the company where ideally the company should be trying to reach out and get in touch with the individual.

We used to train salespeople to value and collect every crumb of information on a client or potential client. They have a kid taking karate classes? Noted. They breed toy poodles? Noted. They're having a rough time in their marriage? Noted. They're thinking about buying a new car?

You get the picture.

At Omega we took this approach so seriously that we required our reps to keep detailed notes about their clients and then we made sure that we tracked it. Building that approach into the system is a huge step for a couple of reasons. Firstly as soon as you have a client list of a couple of hundred or more then it's a rare rep that can keep those details straight in their head and inevitably a lot of the finer detail is lost. Secondly, using your employees' heads for data storage is very dangerous if they change divisions or (perish the thought) leave the company. So we would keep these details in a database so that even a brand new sales rep on a call could note that the client's eldest daughter was due to go for a black belt earlier that month and ask if she had made the grade.

Naturally keeping the notes is only the first part of the process. Simply having reps reel off details from a fact sheet is the sort of thing that should be left to soulless production-line call-centres trying to push printer ink cartridges at bored veal-pen dwellers. Since you intend to have the imagination to go further I'd expect you to use a bit of that vision when it comes to taking those observed details and turning them into a business opening or a relationship builder.

Real building relationships requires going the extra mile and not just noting detail or salting it away but acting on it and truly entering into the spirit of things.

For example, we once had a client who it turned out was a cult follower of *The Rocky*

Horror Picture Show. We even found out that she and her friends would meet for the regular showing in her home town where like-minded folk could get together and do the Time Warp. If you've never been to a fully interactive screening of *Rocky Horror* then you're missing out; the film's own exuberant, camp celebration of B-films and the RKO era of Hollywood would be worth the price of admission, but what makes the evening is the interaction of the audience who will, on cue, fling toast, fire water pistols, cower under newspapers, race to the screen towel in hand, and bellow innuendo. They also tend to be dressed in fishnet stockings, whatever their gender may be.

So one night my wife and I turned up too.

We had a ball and my client was astonished to see that we'd remembered her Dr Frankenfurter fetish (again, if you don't know who I mean then you should go some time). So to cap it off, I went to a local trophy maker and had them make a prize for her. Instead of a cup it featured a rock on a pedestal and a simple inscription dedicated to my client with the words "As Rocky As You Can Get." Simple? Yes. Corny? You might say so – and it would have been if I did that for every client, but this particular person appreciated the fact that I had listened, noted, remembered and gone on to share in that little aspect of her life. After my night at the movies, the volume of business from that client sky-rocketed by over 400%.

Take another example. I once took a potted flower to a client – nothing too unusual in that. She laughed and told me that she was so hopeless with plants that my gift pretty much amounted to a death sentence for the thing. You've probably heard the same or a similar line yourself. Maybe you've found yourself saying it.

We laughed and the moment passed – except that when I got back to the office I made a note on the database. It's a wonderful thing about making notes that the simple fact of doing it really increases your chance of remembering that detail anyway. So when, a couple of months later I was strolling through SoHo in New York and came across a shop selling inflatable potted flowers I remembered her 'brown thumbs' and popped in to buy a couple of them.

Upon returning to Florida, I put them in my office and on the next visit to the city where she worked I found the time to pop by with my collection of "unkillable" plants for her office. She was delighted, and no, I don't think for a moment that it was some little inflatable plant that pleased her so; it was the thought that months after a conversation, and a thousand miles from where it took place, she had still occupied my thoughts and I had chosen to act on that.

Business is about people and as with every area of human interaction it can be the little touches that mean so much to so many.

Which brings me to birthdays. In this day of smartphones and Facebook it's almost harder to forget someone's birthday than to 'remember' it. People are aware that you almost certainly see an electronic reminder of the day they were born and so simply sending an email or a text, while never a bad thing, is not the big deal it once was. Simply firing off an email in return to say 'happy birthday' is the sort of thing that can be (and often is) automated so my thinking is that if you want to show you really remembered, or you actually care then we have to work a little bit harder. That makes saving detail on the little stuff like hobbies and pets that matters all the more important. Plus, if you are going to send a birthday greeting, once again – like the old thank you note – **Don't Ever Forget** to buy a real birthday card and send it via snail mail. As fewer and fewer people do that it acquires all the more charm and becomes a little like a time capsule from an altogether different age.

Which makes you stand out and be remembered in your turn.

I've long cultivated a habit of sending cards or buying little gifts for people when I happen to remember them. It used to be a bit of a joke but turned into a point of pride that I would always say "I probably won't remember your birthday, but don't think that means I don't remember you; and I will periodically prove it." You don't have to have a special reason to get in touch with a client. In fact, no reason at all is probably the very best reason. A card or note sent on the occasion of nothing more than the fact that you're thinking of them or that something has reminded you of them can be all it takes to forge the kind of business and personal rapport that brings success all round.

Do Try This At Home

Think of a customer or business associate that matters to you. Now think of one that might matter to you in the future. How much information do you have about them both? How much could you find out? Get to work – Google them, ask friends, check social networks and see what kind of details you can turn up then make sure you've got a simple and efficient way of storing that information so you can retrieve it again when it might come in handy.

TIM FARGO

PQR
Pursue Quantitative Results

"Define your business goals clearly so that others can see them as you do."

-   George F. Burns

*A goal without a number is just a wish. Worse than that, if you can't tell the difference and you're confusing wishes with goals then you are doomed to wasting your life chasing mirages instead of hitting your targets. This is why you must **Pursue Quantitative Results**.*

Ask any fitness instructor what people say they want from a gym – and why they don't get it. They'll tell you that in almost every induction session new gym goers say their aims are to "lose weight and get fit," which sounds reasonable enough, except that these aren't goals. They're vague concepts and because they aren't pinned to any kind of measurable objective they are almost certain to fail. Personal trainers try to encourage people to start thinking about exactly how much weight, or to think instead of dropping a dress size or going back to wearing 30 inch trousers because these are specific, deliverable goals with a clear metric (means of measurement).

Given a clear-cut goal with specific deliverables and a deadline goal – losing six kilos in six months for example, people are likely to achieve their aims. Without those things they don't and after a while of thrashing around in their new gym they start finding excuses not to go and eventually the gym ends up banking subscription fees from yet another no-show who finds comfort by agreeing with all their friends that gyms don't work.

I'll put my hand up and admit to being a bit of a fitness fanatic. As part of that I keep a daily log of my weight (with a goal of maintaining 75kg) along with the activity performed for the day along with the estimated number of calories burnt, a list of what I ate, and an estimate of the calories that represents. You probably think that's nuts. You wouldn't be the first to say so. Yet to me this seems far less bizarre than all those people who are surprised to find that they've put on weight. If you eat more than you burn – you'll get fat. If you burn more than you eat – you'll get thin. Forget all the nonsense about faddy diets with only eating certain food groups or no carbs in the evening – just use more calories than you put in and you will lose weight. It comes down to simple maths.

The same applies to those other great fake goals – 'getting rich' and 'being successful'. They're not goals, they're wishes, just like 'being fit' and 'losing weight' and if you want to convert them from dreams to goals then you're going to have to set exact way points and ways of measuring.

You wouldn't get into your car without knowing where you intend to go, but when it comes to business and personal success too many of us are effectively driving along, heading nowhere, with no way of knowing where we want to go or how to know if we get there.

Remember when I told my supervisor that if I worked as hard in the private sector as I did working on my PhD I'd be able to retire in ten years? While it certainly sounded confident, that was a wish, not a goal. In order to make this wish a reality, I had to establish a series of goals.

Remember that Ferrari I used to sit in and imagine a day when I could actually own one? Then you probably also remember that I sat down with an Excel spreadsheet and worked out exactly how much money I needed to buy the car. I didn't *wish* to one day own a Ferrari. I sat down and did the math to make it a quantifiable goal.

So we have to pick way points to success,

and that means setting benchmarks.

As I ran Omega, I was constantly evaluating a set of operational metrics against benchmarks that were set by me, not some industry standard. The way I see it, using an industry standard is like studying to be a C student. You don't want to be average, you want to crush the competition. Daily sales was an obviously important metric, but it also had to be evaluated against the current work load (in a service business too much work is nearly as problematic as too little).

In a growing business, the monitoring of cash and the collection of receivables is also critical. More small companies fold due to cash flow problems than profitability. Failure to understand the cash needs of a business as it grows is a terminal illness. You must be able to look at where your money goes – whether through payroll, vendor payments, or other outlays and against that you have to balance how quickly your money will come in.

Having solid goals for the collection of receivables is essential. If the DSO (day sales outstanding) gets too high you will hit a wall. Of course, you also need to secure financing as a method to create a net, so a failure to meet your goal isn't fatal. But you need to be clear that the financing is a safety net, not a mattress. The same went for stretching our outlays of cash. We had mobile phone bills that were over $10,000 per month. We would wait until the last day for timely payment and then pay the bill using a corporate credit card. Not only did we accrue miles to be used for employee contests, we also got an additional thirty to forty five days to pay the bill. We used this approach for every single expense. Why? Because we had a concrete goal of always keeping one month's worth of cash expenditures in reserve. So if an entire month went by without a single soul paying us, we'd still be humming along.

By the time the firm grew big enough to have a solid IT team (and we had fantastic people), I was able to evaluate all our key metrics without having to do more than look at a couple of screens worth of information. I've lost count of the number of CEOs I've met who don't demand this information at their fingertips, but for me, not having visible details of all your cash flow is like flying a plane without a control panel.

Personally, I like to have software that allows you to drill down into individual metrics about every aspect of your business. Does this cost more? Well, yes, but the return on investment is huge.

Being able to measure how productive a given employee is over time is one critical measure. It doesn't necessarily have to be a reason to promote or fire someone, but from **Pursuing Quantitative Results** you create questions. Why are there gaps in their productivity? The knee-jerk reaction is to say they're lazy, but that may be lazy thinking since a closer look may turn up all sorts of elements (logistics for example) that make the same job harder for one branch or worker than for another. In the case of Omega, it paid to keep an equally close eye on the profitability of the clients. Many businesses evaluate clients by volume which is a recipe for disaster.

When we found that a client was not profitable, we tried to sit down with them to renegotiate better pricing. Otherwise we would find that the way they tried to trim costs would end up costing us more. For example, they might switch to half-day surveillance rather than full-day which left our investigators stuck and unproductive in a remote area.

In many ways what **PQR** really means is pursuing the kind of process-driven assessment normally associated with manufacturing – regardless of the business you're in. Process matters, because if you don't know what went into that lovely cake you just baked, you will have a hard time replicating the result. If you have standards around each aspect of how something is done, you can both replicate and improve it.

Examining the details of a job often help understand where costs lie. You might think having someone tailed in a car is pretty straightforward and the costs come in the form of one driver, one car and some fuel. But if you have an aggressive driver they won't take long to notice a tail following them as they weave across lanes. In one case, we found a guy who took four drivers to follow him (often from ahead, or covering off different exit ramps). Turned out he had another job on the side while claiming benefits for not being able to work. The cost of four drivers was more than repaid but it took an understanding of the detail to be able to explain it and recoup it from the client.

Which brings me back to setting goals. Trying to reduce costs in that case by reducing the number of drivers would have made the job impossible because one guy working four times as hard would simply have exposed himself. However, setting four guys on the case got us an answer way faster than having one operative repeatedly losing someone on their daily journey. So again, simple 'wishes' like cost-cutting aren't enough – you have to quantify on a case by case basis where you can do better, and to do that, you have to have the information about what is involved in your business.

Another element of **Pursuing Quantitative**

Results is to set reachable points and in the process break down the big goals into bite-sized pieces. Trying to do too much too soon only leads to frustration and decreases your chances of getting there. For example, if you're working on the issue of DSO, then think about trying to reduce the time money is owed from 40 days to 35. It may not sound like much, but for a $20M dollar business that bite-sized change results in an additional $273,000 in the company's accounts.

Do Try This At Home

Start by drawing up a list of what success looks like. First think what it looks like five or ten years from now, then work backwards so you can start to pick off the steps and the goals that will get you there. Once you're at the stage where you have goals to achieve this year then break them down and think what you will need to do month by month to reach that point. Then week by week. You can see where we're going here, but the point is that if you don't have a goal for just what you're going to do tomorrow to take you to success then why do you think you're going to get there? Not planning for success every day will eventually mean you will find yourself somewhere you didn't expect and wonder how that happened. Just like all those people who one day realise they're ten kilos (22 lbs) more than they were when they were at college.

TIM FARGO

STU
Start Teaching and Understanding

"I have never let my schooling interfere with my education."

- Mark Twain

There are many styles of leadership that work – from inclusive we're-in-this-together approaches to old-fashioned, top-down dictatorship. Personally I like to lead from the front but I'm a great believer that if you want your troops to be right behind you then you'd best know their thinking and have them fully understand yours. That means more than telling people what to do – it means showing them, it means to **Start Teaching and Understanding**.

Telling people what to do is great if you're in the business of bringing up a bunch of minions or lackeys to follow your every order and freeze into panicky immobility at the thought of independent action. Personally I like to be able to count on the people around me and part of that is about showing them what you mean then sharing experiences so you develop mutual understanding. That's as true for trainees as it is for partners, shareholders, and yes, even customers.

Educating customers is one of the great struggles for many businesses. In our own area we found that when we were selling to clients they would often have wildly unrealistic expectations of what we could do. We would spend hours if not days explaining the boundaries of the law, of the resources available to us, and in some cases the limits of human beings being assigned jobs.

After a while we noticed that a lot of the misunderstandings about what we did were common to pretty much all clients and so we hit on the idea of a media campaign to explain our abilities and manage expectations. The result was a booklet called "Claimants, Lies and Videotape" which we then took on the road to trade shows with a booth rigged up to look like a movie marquee showing "Claimants, Lies and Videotape" and starring Omega Insurance Services.

The results weren't bad but it was clear that there was a hesitance to commit to learning about us so we asked around to find out what it was that might encourage potential customers commit to learning more about the services they were thinking of hiring.

The answer turned out to be the continuing

education credits that are required in most states. So we got to work to get our seminar approved in every state where we had clients. More than that though, we even began a programme to educate people about our programme to educate people. This took the form of a PR campaign with articles in national publications both print and online. It's not enough to do something well, you have to make some noise about it, and to really be appreciated you have to be ready to show people just what it is you do and what it is about how you do it that makes you so special.

Which brings me to training.

Teaching your customers what you're about is a great way of increasing sales but it all counts for nothing if you fail to deliver on the promise. Ensuring that your company can deliver comes down to the people you hire, and the way you teach them. Which means training and just about every company CEO you ever meet will nod wisely at the mention of the word and tell you just how important training is and what a lot of trouble they go to for the sake of their staff.

Except they don't. At least not in my experience.

Instead, what most companies mean by 'training' is better described as cramming a bunch of newbies into a room then boring them into submission with a monotone lecturer who believes that if one PowerPoint slide is good then 100 must be so much better. You can't teach people to understand a job and a way of thinking by lecturing them – you have to drag them out there into the big wide world and show them what just you mean.

Theory is all well and good but for pretty much every line of business, the hardest things to teach are attitude and judgement, and that's precisely what you want to encourage if you're going to foster a can-do culture around you.

There's an old test used in a number of secret services in which the trainer takes trainees to a street, points out a randomly-chosen balcony, and tells them their mission is to find their way onto it. How they do it is up to them – they could ring the door bell and talk their way in as someone who used to live there, they could pretend to be the gas man, or they can do their very best Spider-man impersonation. What matters is seeing how they approach the task, how resourceful they are, and how well their personality adapts to new demands.

We don't actually get our people to make their way onto strangers' balconies, but we do run a little test where we get trainees to phone people randomly-selected from the phone book and find out just what information they can glean from them during a call. The smarter candidates quickly realise that a combination of a good cover story and a friendly phone manner will get them to details of a stranger's life that straight questioning never will. It's not something most people start off feeling relaxed with, but you can see those with the ability to think on the move and wing their way to results. It's far better than teaching them how to do it in a classroom and seeing how well they regurgitate your messages.

As for field investigators, we like to put them through the mill before they even start formal training. Regardless of their background or level of experience we would send them out with one of our old hands so they could get a feel for the way we liked to work and we could get a feel for how well they adapted to it.

There's nothing glamorous about field investigation. Anyone who thinks it's like Humphrey Bogart casing a joint with a quart of bourbon and an obliging brunette will be flattened by the odd mix of boredom and adrenaline. Boredom because you can spend hours sitting in a car waiting for nothing to happen. Adrenaline because when things happen they can happen in a hurry, and if people suddenly want to know what the hell you're doing you can find yourself facing some pretty raw hostility.

The nature of the job often takes investigators to far flung places where frankly they'd rather not be. On top of that, being there requires a pretty good cover story about what you're doing. If you're tailing someone in a rural neighbourhood it takes a fair amount of nerve to explain, unblinkingly, that you're sitting in a car all day because you're studying the mating and migration of the Canadian Speckle Headed Warbler. And the nature of life means that chances are if you do come out with that line you're going to find you're talking to an experienced ornithologist. Investigators don't need the driving skills of Steve McQueen and the gun hand of Billy the Kid – they need a cool head, quick wits and the patience of a tortoise learning to ice skate.

So you don't tell people what to expect, you show them.

One instance that sticks in the mind was a prospect who went out with an investigator on a boiling hot summer day in a Florida neighbourhood that was sweaty in more ways than one. The investigator opened the windows but cut the engine (a car with a running engine is sure to attract attention) and with it the AC. The old hand took out some chilled towels from a cooler and passed one to the prospect but the new guy was still getting visibly uncomfortable after only a few minutes. So our man took out an empty bottle he had to hand and explained he was about to use it to relieve himself (not pretty but normal practice for long stake-outs where you can't get out of the car).

This was too much for our would-be gumshoe who was out of the car and onto the pavement before you could zip a fly.

You don't actually have to have employees peeing in bottles to make your point, you just have to know your own business well enough to understand what's really involved and then make sure you expose your trainees to that aspect just as much as you tell them about the good times. Of course, it's not always a disagreeable job for our employees. From time to time it did happen that the person being checked up on was a female employee claiming disability while secretly working as an exotic dancer. Curiously we never had a shortage of male investigators ready to hang out in bars and do the homework on that sort of job, but that wasn't the experience I was interested in showing to trainees. I'd rather they understand the harder edge of a business and to do that I had to know what was involved myself.

The other part of hiring that I've always insisted on is a Happy Hour for the prospective salespeople, myself, and some of the managers and fellow workers. Why would you buy drinks for someone you might not even hire? Because socialising is part of the business, as is letting your hair down in a controlled way, and I only hire people who I think I can trust to do both.

It's curious what happens when people lose

their ambitions. I don't just mean the ones who lose it completely and mumble about their mothers before going to make friends with the toilet, no I mean some of the attitudes that come out. I remember one candidate who I was chatting with when a hockey game came on TV. He literally turned his back to me and started watching the game and continued drinking the beer that we were paying for. I like hockey as much as the next guy but I think that anyone who loses the context of where and what they are doing like that would be better off working somewhere where they aren't expected to keep their wits about them. Another potential candidate confided that he only really wanted the job as a stop-gap while he was trying to break into the porno business. It's an unusual gambit for someone who is, effectively, in a job interview and not one that I would recommend. I have no idea if he lived his dream and is working in the skin trade but he certainly never got to work at Omega. You might think it odd that I choose to check people out by plying them with drink, or leaving them parked in a car all day but I can promise you that I learned more about them, and they learned more about what I was about. That's something we wouldn't get from a straight month of theory lectures.

Do Try This At Home

A lot of companies have specialised departments which is good, but those departments often impact on the running of other departments, and if they don't understand each other you have a recipe for friction. So why not try job-sharing schemes, job shadowing for trainees in different departments or even job-showcasing where workers get together (be prepared to pay for drinks and nibbles) and explain what it is they *really* do.

VWX
Value With X-factor

"A good plan violently executed now is better than a perfect plan executed next week."

- George S Patton

Everything you do should be based around the simple question of "does it add value to my business – or not?" Whether choosing a company or deciding how much to spend on paper clips, there is no other question that matters. Get that sense of value going in a company and you'll be amazed the talent you can inspire. And above all, always **Value With X-factor**.

One day our corporate controller came into my office for a meeting. Now I don't think he was actually banging the table or beating up the furniture, but for whatever reason half way through the discussion the faceplate of a drawer on my desk fell off and we found ourselves both looking down at it. The corporate controller immediately offered to get me another desk. I said "Bob, just get me some glue, I don't see a new desk generating any additional profits for the company."

Too many decisions are made based on satisfying ego. We're all very creative when it comes to dressing up the demands of our own egos in fetching little rationalised disguises. So the reason we need that luxury car is not about ourselves, but all about reflecting the status of the company. The reason we have to travel first class is that it is expected of a successful businessman and we will arrive less tired thereby saving any money spent in terms of our increased productivity. Sometimes that's true, but really we all know what happens to our judgement when people are given the chance to spend 'company' money rather than our own.

It's the same mentality that leads to the kind of spats and internal warfare that spring up about who has the biggest office or the best location. I've heard of employees breaking out the tape measures to establish that one. I've also met managers who like to encourage that kind of rivalry on the basis that it fosters a spirit of competition which keeps employees on their toes and encourages ambition. I'm really not so sure about that – I can't help but feel personally that every ounce of energy being used up in that kind of rivalry is energy that's not being used to drive the company forward.

At Omega I tried the opposite tack. I would encourage people to cut corners not because we were short on money or I had a mean streak, but because I like a mentality that's totally focussed on the business and which gets away from the idea of company money and resources as a bottomless pit of 'perks'.

So we got involved in some little motivating competitions of our own – it's just that they were the exact opposite of the kind of contests you might expect.

We would encourage a rolling competition amongst the investigators and the sales reps to see who could find the cheapest hotel room for that week. There was big kudos involved in this since the sales reps liked to see themselves as being the masters of driving a bargain, while the investigators prided themselves on their ability to find what others could not. Put those two groups up against each other and you find there are some incredibly cheap rooms out there if you're prepared to look for them. Of course, it probably also meant a lot of hotels across the States are still talking about those private-eye guys who show up and ask to sleep in the broom closet or the kitchen.

I know it also led to a whole load of different tactics, including those who gambled on taking an upmarket room and finding something to complain about in such a way that they would get a reduction or be 'comped' so they got a free night. In the bizarre poker stakes of the cheap room contest, there was never any doubt that a freebie in a smart hotel trumps even the cheapest flophouse broom closet.

The same logic applied to conferences. Since attending a conference together was a team event we would book several people into a room. The aim was to keep the focus on the job to be done and to my mind assigning luxury rooms to individuals sends out exactly the opposite message to that. Of course, there are a couple of rules to be followed if you want this approach to work.

The first is that you have to be 100% clear that this is not just about being a skinflint. The best way to do that is to make it obvious that when expenditure is about team building; including drinks, food, and partying generally, then the company is ready to hand over hard cash without hesitation.

The second is that the only way this works is if it applies to everyone – no exceptions – and that meant me too when it came to booking rooms and sharing conditions.

If you're reading this and thinking that it's just a sharp way to cut business expenses then you're not completely wrong, but you're missing the best part of the deal. Where this approach really pays off is not counted in monthly outgoings. Instead it's about the mentality it forges amongst staff and that certain star quality – the X factor – that bubbles to the top when people come together and really strive for a common goal.

By encouraging initiative, a can-do culture, and above all the sense that everyone is braving the waves in the same boat, the little examples I've just mentioned help build a much more two-fisted approach to getting things done. Ongoing competitions that test initiative and creativity can be very empowering and, in particular, encourage people to plan on the fly rather than rely on a schedule of meetings, analysis, debate, and finally (belatedly) implementation. There's too much 'paralysis by analysis' in business, meaning that companies are so afraid of making mistakes, and individuals are so averse to risk that new ideas and projects get bogged down in energy-sapping, fear-driven rounds of discussion. I'm not saying that you shouldn't think before you act, but it's also true that you can sit at a desk and rework the permutations of a plan until the sun stops rising. Sometimes, maybe even most times, it's better by far to grab the two or three people involved, sketch it all out on the back of a napkin, and get plans off the ground right away.

Your competitors aren't standing around

waiting for you to fall over. They're looking to get out in front and take your business from you. So you have to be always on the lookout for ways to get a march on them in return. You can't be complacent in today's markets and where once a market leader could look forward to decades of dominance, it's now hard enough to stay ahead for more than a few months. This is where a culture with a tight team of can-do implementers counts for more than any number of vast, mirror-glass buildings filled full of procedurally-minded Muppets.

So at Omega, we valued the X-factor that would ensure we continued to stand out and we never once presumed that we could leave our competitors behind. Now you might think that for an investigating company this meant focussing on catching even more frauds and cheats. Which it did, but if you really create a culture in which everyone looks to add value to the company then the X-factor can come from unexpected directions.

Like the waterworks.

Remember what I call the 'waterworks' (from **DEF**)? Well, one of the reasons why I believe that you should reward everyone's efforts is that they reward you right back and the IT division of our own waterworks services did just that.

Somebody got the idea that we had a lot of

video that we took on investigations and we could do a lot more with it. So the IT division came up with the brilliant idea of our very own YouTube of the best bits for own clients. The result was "Click, You're Busted" which was a username/password protected rogue's gallery of videos that clients could access. It was a huge success because it was eye-grabbing and entertaining on the one hand (if you've ever watched one of those TV shows based on police video you'll know what I mean) but also a serious showcase of what we were capable of proving – plenty of sizzle AND plenty of steak.

You might think that's a long stretch from encouraging people to find cheap rooms, but actually it's not since the bottom line is all about getting the most value from the minimum outlay. Our people were in the habit of looking around for what extra magic we could rustle up from the resources available.

Then someone hit on the idea that if FedEx can do an automated tracking system to let you know just where your packages are at any given time then why couldn't we have an instant update system for our own clients? They log on and get access to completely up to date information on just what's happening and how far we've progressed. That made perfect sense since it brought together the culture of measuring performance at every stage on the way (see **PQR**) and combining that with the idea of excellence through value. Then we went a step further and built an automated system to log client complaints and ensure they were being dealt with (take another look at **DEF** to remind yourself of the importance of speaking to clients – especially unhappy ones). The system featured a timer that would automatically push the problem up a level if it wasn't dealt with within a set period. If it wasn't settled in 72 hours it made its way to me. I'm very happy to say I never once had a problem get that far.

Do Try This At Home

When did you last organise a competition in your company? Or reward anyone other than sales reps who met targets? What message does that send out? So think about the core values for the company and then think about a competition that will make that point. Competitions aren't just about encouraging ambition – if they're done right then they are also a fantastic way of drumming home a message about what it is you think should be rewarded. Don't just do it once a year either – if it's a message you want people to remember every day then they should see that this theme is always there as part of their lives.

YZ
Yellow Zebra

"If you don't get noticed, you don't have anything."

- Leo Burnett

*It's not enough to be good at what you do – you have to be seen to be good at what you do. That means standing out enough that people notice you and in the media blizzard of today's business world it takes a lot to get people to look twice at anything. Bring in the **Yellow Zebra**.*

I've never actually dressed up as a **Yellow Zebra**, but I have come close.

Many years ago I arranged a scavenger hunt for some corporate sponsors and needed some way of generating publicity for it. The hunt involved a degree of fancy dress so I had the idea to rent a Tim-sized banana costume, grab a pair of roller blades, and publicise it in person. Of course I also took the precaution of telling the local press that the idiot behind the whole thing was about to put in an appearance in the local park dressed as an oversized yellow fruit on wheels.

I lost count of how many people told me

they couldn't believe I was going to go and make a fool out of myself like that, but as I saw it, all I had to do was roller blade around for two hours and put up with a lot of jokes about banana skins. To be honest, I didn't really have a whole lot of money to play with for promotion and I needed to make some noise about the event to generate interest and attract enough competitors to keep the sponsors happy.

As it happened it worked a like a treat. Talk to anyone in newspapers about what gets a story onto the page and they'll agree that unless you happen to pick the day man lands on Mars then a picture of someone doing something bananas is pretty much all you need. Especially for the business pages which are otherwise filled entirely with photos of the man-in-suit-holding-giant-cheque variety. In this case, it worked like a bomb and all it took was the will-power to put pride aside for a little while and dare to stand out a little.

Too many times a good idea doesn't make the grade because people don't shout about it enough. Or they suffer the paralysis of analysis and over-think the problem. That leads them to conclude that they need some really sophisticated promotional experience and either the idea dies there or they end up blowing large budgets on professional marketing services. Which is fine if you have the money to blow, but not so much if you don't.

My feeling is that you really don't need to overcomplicate the act of standing out simply because so many people are so afraid to do so at all. Which means that you only need to be a little bit different from the herd to make a lot of impact.

In the early days of Omega, we used to send out postcards because firstly postcards are cheaper to send than a letter and secondly they don't have to be opened which means everyone who comes into contact with them will get the message.

We ran with a theme of these guys in suits from the 1950s looking deadly serious and explaining their problems to each other – to which the reply was along the lines of "Gee, Hank, it's time to turn to Omega."

Cheesy? You bet.

Cheap? Check.

But people got a laugh of it during dull mornings and the cards, with our trademark red and black corporate colours stuck out so much that people still remember that campaign years later.

It's easy to get hung up on issues of brand values and awareness, but frankly a lot of marketing misses the mark because people forget that all you're really doing is shouting "Hey, look at me!" at anyone within earshot. If your product or service is worth looking at, then how you get a customer's attention matters a lot less than the fact of getting it.

We had a sophisticated online tracking system that let clients review case progress and let us know who mattered in the client company. When it came to mail-outs to those people we could have just fired off emails, but then they would have been lost in the daily data deluge. So we went onto e-Bay and bought a couple of hundred clunky old telephones (remember them? With dials and everything?), cleaned them up and sent them out. Each one had a label pointing out how much communications had moved on since those phones, and suggesting how Omega could take them on to the next level.

It worked, and we got a great response.

Another example was that we were always sending out surveillance video to clients so we started to send out bags of microwaveable popcorn to go with them. We even kept a record of the preferred flavour for each client. It didn't cost much, and it made us memorable while helping to refresh the relationship with established clients. That one proved so popular that it wasn't long before a bunch of our rivals started doing the same thing...and you know what they say about imitation being the sincerest form of flattery.

Conferences are a classic example of time to reach for the **Yellow Zebra** factor. A conference is like being dropped into a frothing sea of rival companies all competing for the attention of tired and stressed attendees. The problem is how to stand out like some kind of lighthouse so everyone makes a beeline for you. If you've got the money then you make sure you have the biggest stand and you deck it out with pretty girls and fast cars and whatever else you think will make the average customer stop and stare.

But if you don't have the money?

I remember a conference in Alabama where we found ourselves booked into a booth the size of a shoebox in one of those forgotten aisles that look like they should have tumble weeds blowing through. Of course, you get what you pay for so what can you do? Well, as it happens, I noticed that our booth technically stuck out into the walking area and since the conference was about risk management I promptly suggested to the organisers that we represented a fire hazard. Since there were no other stands available I suggested we set up in the registration area which had no facilities for fancy stands but was, of course, absolutely heaving with people coming and going. We got the space, and we got a huge amount of attention with it all because we weren't shy about shouting out about ourselves.

Another time at the soberly-titled Florida

95

Worker's Compensation Annual Meeting we thought we'd help put a bit of bite into the whole thing by creating our very own Mardi Gras. We mixed and served 'Hurricanes' (check out Pat O'Brien's New Orleans bar for the original recipe) and started throwing out Omega medallions and beads with all the enthusiasm of a fraternity house turning up at, well, Mardi Gras. A few people were worried that we'd get in trouble for that but I've always worked on the principle that it's better to seek forgiveness than ask permission, and besides, there was nothing in the exhibitor rulebook that actually forbade it. So from negotiating our way out of one spot for being a fire hazard we certainly did a good job of becoming one this time around. Not only the attendees, but most of our competitors, ended up jammed solid around our booth jumping up and down to get their share of booze and beads. I think it was fair to say that absolutely nobody who was there expected to have so much fun at the Florida *Worker's Compensation Annual Meeting*.

A side benefit of this was that the staff just loved working the shows and because they were fired up about things it gave our booths a buzz that the others didn't have. I'm a firm believer that working hard doesn't mean you can't be having fun and that clients respond to that no matter how 'serious' your business. As part of that, we also had a rule that anyone working on a booth had to be standing up at all times and preferably doing their best impersonation of a fairground barker standing outside the tent of the Tattooed Lady. If anyone didn't want to be calling on the customers to roll up then they shouldn't have been there and that attitude goes a long way to standing out when you're surrounded by a sea of grey suits.

The key here is not just to act the fool to make people stare. It's not enough to catch a customer's eye – you also have to communicate your message and capture their data. Way too often that data capture consists of a sad-looking goldfish bowl that people drop business cards into because they might win something. Instead of that we would always find a reason why potential customers should fill in a short questionnaire (for the importance of this take another look at **MNO**).

When it comes to the **Yellow Zebra** factor, undoubtedly the biggest mistake of most businesses is failing to stand out in the first place. The second biggest mistake, however, is getting to first base by attracting all that attention, but then failing to convert that into any kind of real sales conversation. If you're just providing the **Yellow Zebra** without any meaningful follow up then you're not a businessman; you're an entertainer.

Do Try This At Home

So what is it about your company that stands out to an observer? Your product? Your pricing? Your logo? What's the **Yellow Zebra** factor for your business? What would make you walk straight up to your company's stand if you were a stranger walking around a packed conference or trade show? Does the same factor work as well online as it does in person? Would a potential customer recognise that **Yellow Zebra** factor whenever they came into contact with your company? If you're not sure about the answers to this, then it's time to start scribbling on the back a napkin, or grab the two most creative people you know and brainstorm until your grey matter hurts. Be sure of one thing – a business that fails to stand out won't be standing on its own two feet for long.

Reviewing Alphabet Success

In the event that you didn't **Make Notes and Observations** as you read this book, I thought this would be a good opportunity to take one last look at my Alphabet Success before signing off. The first thing is to **Always Be Committed**.

ABC

Don't look at your dreams and goals as half-full/half-empty glasses, but rather drinking horns, vessels that can't be put down once they're picked up. This kind of commitment always keeps you where you need to be so that you **Don't Ever Forget** what's important.

DEF

What is important is telling the people who are helping you to achieve your goals how much you appreciate them. This includes the people who complain the most, because at least they're sharing their opinions rather than just walking away. Thanking everyone is one of the many ways of **Getting Highly Inspired**, not only yourself, but those around you.

GHI

And those around you aren't going to be excited about what they're doing if you can't do the same. Getting Highly Inspired keeps you going strong and helps you to **Just Keep Looking** for new opportunities to bring your A game to everything you do.

JKL

New opportunities bring new challenges and obstacles, and it's paramount you're constantly paying attention to finding different ways around them. And a great way to stay focussed is to **Make Notes and Observations.**

MNO

Little details bring with them huge values. Taking notes and remembering things that are important to others can be the secret to success, especially in terms of maintaining relationships with your clients and employees. This'll certainly be a big help as you **Pursue Quantitative Results**.

PQR

It's easier to make a wish than it is to

achieve a goal. What's essential is to not confuse the two. When you say you want to be successful, that's a wish. Now how do you make that wish a reality? Establish quantifiable goals and work your way to achieving your dreams one step at a time. As you move steadily forward, use this time to **Start Teaching and Understanding**.

STU

There are lots of ways to lead, but the best way to have a team working with you is to understand what they are thinking. If you want them to make your dream a reality, it's often good to know what dreams they have. By teaching them your ideas rather than simply telling them, this allows you and your team to **Value With X-factor** when opportunities present themselves down the line.

VWX

Does the decision you've just made bring real value to your company? Or is it satisfying your ego? It's important to understand this difference and set an example for others. Especially when there's a **Yellow Zebra** involved.

YZ

Standing out from the crowd is getting harder and harder to do in today's business world. But by following this Alphabet Success and taking risks – even if it means embarrassing yourself in the process – you'll have a better chance at getting noticed, like a Yellow Zebra. Playing it safe certainly has its own rewards, but you'll just be another person in the crowd until you take a chance.

ABOUT TIM FARGO

Tim Fargo was born outside Buffalo, NY and adopted at three months old. He grew up in Akron, Ohio as a distinctly average kid and moved straight to Florida upon graduating high school in pursuit of a more entertaining environment. After forays into the exotic world of security guard, lifeguard, night auditor, shoe salesman and a myriad of other lucrative professions, he decided to improve his prospects by attending Miami-Dade Community College. Four years later he exited the Florida university system with a B.B.A. from Florida Atlantic University. After bouncing around the business world in some slightly higher paying positions, and a long stint of travel in Mexico and Central America, he ended up faced with the prospect of starting his own business. Less than seven years later he retired. *Alphabet Success* is the product of that unusual journey.

Tim now spends his time between four continents largely having fun but occasionally allowing work to intrude on his day.

Made in the USA
Middletown, DE
15 January 2015